flicker

flicker

____

LISA BICKMORE

ELIXIR PRESS
DENVER, COLORADO

FLICKER. Copyright © 2016 by Lisa Bickmore. All rights reserved. Printed in the United States of America. For information, address Elixir Press, PO Box 27029, Denver, CO 80227.

www.elixirpress.com

Cover art, "Scattered Light," by Jim Campbell.
Photo, "Scattered Light at Northern Spark," by Tony Webster.
Author photo by David Bisson
Book design by Steven Seighman

Library of Congress Cataloging-in-Publication Data
Bickmore, Lisa Orme, 1957-
[Poems. Selections]
Flicker / Lisa Bickmore.
    pages ; cm ISBN 1-932418-57-1 (alk. paper)
I. Title.
PS3552.I318A6 2015 811'.54—dc23
                        2015012783

10   9   8   7   6   5   4   3   2   1

for my parents

and

for John

TABLE OF CONTENTS

*You are the stream, the fish, the light,
the pulsing shadow*

—DENISE LEVERTOV

flicker

Sutra

I wanted a leaner, a sparer style.

I wanted birds to be able to fly
through the branches
after the pruning.

In a chastened season,
why my longing,
appearing everywhere?

> *on the walk, fallen*
> *   crabapples   smear of ochre*
> *crushed under heel*

Conundrum to be solved by *techné,*
I thought, though perhaps

I loomed larger:
I wanted to be the altar,
not to kneel there.

Concord

at leaf lift, fat fruit falling
         to hand, bubble-headed bird
                  secrets glass-blown
hard seed heart, tongue-crushed

sweet bloom-end narcissi, sugar holding
         scent-heavy fence brambler,
                  branch brawny shoulders,
         twiggy hands, mouth of its violet

kiss—or even darker, a velvet sheen
         pearl or nacre first snow-
                  gleam glove-cleared, rubbed,
         thumb-polished, this

untended flower mouth bee-stung
         berry, this love honey tumble
                  sweet thicket, autumnal
         tendril, unmeditated

yield; this nonetheless late gleaning,
         a transcendental century
                  and a half hence its cold Massachusetts
         roots, declension of vitis Labrusca,

black fox grape the native wilding,
         frontier now of my tillage, my
                  viticulture, my clean Ball jars,
         my Northern thrift, my lyric

husbandry—plump bushels all this unbroken
         afternoon sheared from vine and cane:
                  swoon plummy and beguiled
         into my marveling palms—

In my old book

                    there are two lives,
the tranquil one and the conflagration.
Wildflower seeds exploded there
with the flicked matches I walked away from.
I drove with an engine gunning
for no destination but *fly*. My head on fire.
I liked it hot. My body a combustible room—
the twitch in my thighs rifled, my arms

incendiary. My vow to a many-named god
—*flicker* the name of the red-cheeked
bird that swooped through my meadow
flutter how my heart did beat when
it did not *flail* instrument I used
for penance: ritual constant as flame.
My steady prayer a secret I kept
even from myself.
                    Now, long
after I'd finished all this—I believed
I was through with it—still I carry
the coals of it in my breast. Every morning
I stoke it, I kneel—if not there,
I don't know where to start.
You won't believe the streaks
of ash on my knees.

From a Pastoral

For the white secret of their underwings;
for the patterns of their markings,
which gather them together in clans;
for the dusky sky which has spilt its roses,
the wild sunflowers tall as saplings,
the wind picking up and carrying on;
for gulls alighting on a field just plowed,
for small planes landing, and the slow descent
of parachutes into the late western light;
for color that darkens into nothing in shadow,
brightening to nothing in light;
for enigmatic water in canals and ditches,
cutting through the palimpsest of suburbs
over old farmland; for haven in change,
in moving on; and for the morning,
when the sky lightens like a milky stone
over the old sugar factory road, and the lightning
daring to go everywhere; for the luck of this,
for my lack which turns to starved sight, draws
near to birds, ministers of dawn and dark,
pieces reckless music out of the sky.

Descant

What does winter abolish, its icy scroll
unrolling over an old rough text?
At the corner under the street lamp,

the light at nine snows down to the walk.
The four o'clocks have withdrawn into blackness.
Meanwhile, Federico Garcia Lorca waits for me

on the porch. I have been expecting him:
he has prophesied his own coming
in my dreams, his eyes filled with an oceanic light.

This evening, he comes as a flame-colored cat.
He will not acknowledge me, implying everything
in the disdainful curve of his spine.

I have ignored him one time too many.
When I hail him, his tail switches rudely,
his haunches settle. His back is striped green,

though, the sure sign. I follow him
as he leaps from the doorstep
to the ground below, then to the orchard

behind the house, where withered pears
still hang from the trees. The leaves
have not all fallen. I see the cat there

for a last moment before he vanishes.
My children still perch in the branches
telling riddles. I am wild to be near them,

to hear their hushed words.

In Memphis

In the rage and desire of lapsed Christians,
from their exhausted mornings, the worship of lack;
from the dust heaps of recursion,
and the waste, the flowering pears undone,

it shall be you, Nashville, of Tennessee,
of red square buildings smudged with smoke,
of the square schools and church houses of vintages unknown:
Tennessee of U.S. Interstate 40 to Memphis, in March,
of raw trees, red tipped;

it shall be you, abandoned cinemas and historical markers,
ministers of congregations past,
of faded prayers and hymn singing;

you, Cumberland river, many bridged;
the road cut into strata of rock,
all night restaurants and cocktail lounges;

you, the plunder of hotel rooms
where there is no sleep; cups of coffee,
cups of wine, spilled, swallowed, tasted or not tasted;

it shall be you, old dark horse grazing peaceably,
acreage, pasture, hills, red wasps of meditation,
the names of a thousand lovers and revilers scratched

into the brick at the gates, the white gates of Graceland.

Thaumaturge

The dead bird—or rather the bird's
robes, scattered as if it had

been forcibly undressed,
rise and drift back down at my foot-

stir. The cat rests on the high back
of the easy chair at the window,

striped, tigerish. Most mornings
she cozies up in the chairnook,

feathers the blanket,
though daily she also tears

down the hall through the kitchen
and back, when she finds

the twitch of her own tail
unbearable, provoking.

It's almost mouse season,
the field in back her field,

where she flees for all
the warm hours, returning

with a fat, a small, a young,
a worn one to dismantle on the tile,

leaving only a dark density
of organs as evidence.

But the bird: the bird she ate
down to the last sticky bit

at the end of one feather.
Up high, she adorns

the chair back, looks into the sun,
the bird's heart a power inside her.

Letter to Cuerpo de Paz

April, West Jordan

Every afternoon, your letter says, the rain
falls. Before or after your running,
I wonder? You used to smoke cigarettes
outside our building, and I chided you, dearest
Jen, urged you to stop, my rhetorical
ploy to offer you almonds and chocolate.

That thing you have going with chocolate
and almonds? fucking great! you write. The rain
hasn't fallen here, really, for months. No rhetorical
spin possible there—water running
low and lower—every drop in the garden dear
as silver. The camaraderie of cigarettes

maybe means you still smoke Marlboro Lights
with new friends. I'd rather you ate chocolate,
whatever kind they have there. *You can't commandeer*
water here, you write, *no matter how much rain—*
at least not clean water, in wells or running
in pipes. Here, even with "conserve water" rhetoric,

we waste it on lawns—the English garden trope.
We disbelieve our desert, despite the light
each evening, purples and pinks running
water-colored over the mountains, faced in mocha,
iced with snow. Now, early warmth means even the rain
and snow of last winter won't bring a dearly

needed wet year. Meanwhile, cariña,
I assume you're immersed in a new rhetoric:
of children in their underwear who dance in the rain,
of erratic electricity, sporadic light,
of new spellings for smoke, persuasion, chocolate,
and the constant syntax of running.

They of the village interpret your daily run,
but you're a missionary, a darling
stranger, the runner to whom they offer chocolate,
their only aim pleasure, with no implied demand:
I was a pedant then, when you lit up,
but now, on spring afternoons gusting with rain,

I like to think of you, fleet dear, running, breath
and muscle the only rhetoric, without smoke
or chocolate, in an absence of the absence of rain.

Girl

A junkie stands outside the blood bank, where no one gives blood,
though he just has, apparently, and looks the colder for it.

I am flying through this January night, driving fast
through the dark hours, past the window, UTAH BLOOD BANK, past

the chairs in gray rows of cracked leatherette, as if you could
strap in and blast off, concentrate on flight and space and not

on the blood like rivers going into cold storage. He
is a hungry boy and needs someone to cook him something

(to eat, perchance to nod . . .), although the boy is here, my dark
rastafari, and you are not, and though once you said to me

get in this bed, now you're gone, elsewhere, on your way. The night
smells like yeast, bread rising and baking in a penumbral

panederia full of bread, sugared rolls shaped like dream dogs
and rabbits and pale horses, and soft sopaipillas

(let me fry this bread for you, puffed into pillows and sweet
with honey); still, it's only just Cordova's El Rancho,

cooking the scraps for the last late diners; so let me shuck
oysters for you instead, two dozen of them, all set round

a pretty plate, and, for your old decadence, pour a glass
of fumet blanc. No? Then I will stop and order triple

espresso cappuccino caffelatte deluxe, which
I will bring to wake you up, tear you out of this absence

in which you flourish, where you go on without me
in this sacrament, this blood and bread for no one, though I cry

your name to your deafness, into some geography,
some lost city where, at an anonymous grill, there stands

thc back and neck of you, dressed in white, cooking hamburgers
in the splendor, the waste and hunger of America.

In Taos

—that town famous for disappearances, its fences and pueblos,
where they have no mail because no addresses,
town of the fried potatoes laced with fragrant grease
and chile verde, where your father mudded the old chicken coop,
doused it in white paint and called it a house,

where you lived, where you slept in late every morning
as was your custom, where you did not work and where you wrote
long letters scrawled over the image of your face on the paper,
emerging like the stigmata, burning eyes, mouth full of fire,

where the letters pile up in the corners of the post office,
the post office de los ultimos dias,
the post office de los desaparecidos,
forlorn letter carriers drifting about in the desolate snow,
finding one after another letter undeliverable
in the place I could have gone, I could have gone with you:

though in that case it would no longer be this Taos,
town over the mountains with no addresses,
this town of fried potatoes and chicken coops and paint
and stigmata and chile and sleep and snow and rain
and moon stars white sun: it would, finally,

be where we lost one another, where I'd stay,
having given up everything, everything in this world,
to be there, the marks of this village burned like dry wood,
smoke, embers and ashes on my skin, my envelope,
stamped, canceled, and therefore, nowhere.

The Gate

The house daily heaps its opulence
on the board: pears, peaches, plums.
Jars full of alyssum. Three rosebuds
so tightly folded their fragrance is green.
Behind the fence there's a long field with a road;
beyond that, the far hills. The early sun
across the valley extends its hand
to ignite the west windows.

The mother watches the boy out the back gate
in the morning, with his friend or sometimes alone.
Down the road a little he finds the rope swing
by the canal, at the shining poplar,
a tree that likes to talk, when the wind picks up.
He hears its leaves and a barely audible tune
whistled far down the road. He swings across the canal.
He moves with the rope in his hands;

he gets a lift from the south wind,
repeating but not exhausting the motion.
The sun makes the day's half-loop.
Light rages in the late hills, and he turns back.
He'd like his mother to come, or his dad,
to see the place, maybe test the swing.
In his skinny abraded arms lies the long shape
of the rope, the hard knots. On his feet

a faintly muddy over-layer where
the water skimmed the soles. He comes back
through the gate like a small myth, his gold head,
green eyes glowing, animate. At the table
he eats the meal before him; placing it there,
the mother pats his princely head as she turns.
Later the sky hangs out its cold disk,
with the hammer marks of the silversmith.

He sleeps in soft blankets. Down the hall,
the man and the woman, his parents,
by now past journeying, lie together
and apart in their bed, opening and closing
like a gate. Through it, tonight, walks a younger
child, the boy when he was small. He struggles
from within a dream and cries out,
No, I don't want you to leave! It wounds

them all to hear, to know what he knows.

Ring of Fire

In *Rolling Stone* there's an old photograph of them
flushed with love, standing by an airplane at Heathrow,

slim bags like dogs at heel. Was she still married at the time?
Was he? Every thing ends—country songs, stanzas,
marriages. Once, mind astray, I said aloud what I feared

—that I must repent. To this exhausted thought
a friend replied, *You must tell yourself,*

that may be right, but I can't think about it just now.
I wondered: *and if the fire goes wild?*
He first met her backstage, said *One day I'll marry you.*

She laughed. *Good, I can't wait*, and prayed for years,
him speeding toward her, then away. She might have said,

You may be right, but I really can't think about it just now.
She wrote the song her sister sang first
in a guileless voice. When he woke in a sweat,

he heard it, mariachi horns fading from his dream.
His voice inimitable, resonant;

the bass thrumming and the horns a surreal,
jaunty punch between chorus and verse. Like prayer,
despair of two different orders surging in the voices,

dire hunger, no matter the version.
On *Classic Cash*, which I bought

during those years when they were both
still alive, he repeats the last chorus twice,

and then the last line once more—
That ring of fire, that ring of fire. A year
after he died, at last I heard her own recording.

She grew up on mountain music, which sometimes
has an uneven measure. So her song finishes sooner,

one less beat at each verse-end. And now
I hear in her rougher alto sighing *Oh,*
I fell into her specific form of rue.

Borrowed Tune

too wasted to write my own
Neil Young

There is a music of engines and rain,
derived and derived again, tires on a road
after dark. The train hurtles along I-10,

I see it before I see him, dim figure
at the roadside waiting for a break
in the breath and whine of cars. My voice

entered a song when last I was that transient,
ready vagabond if the traffic would slow,
to catch a ride anywhere: there is a thread

attached to his heart I pull patiently,
steadily, to hear it again. Even then
I knew I'd borrow this tune over

and over—just dark desert, a train, just
lightning inscribing runes on the sky,
highway lines etched in broken streaks of blue.

It is older than my memory,
but I use it anyway: driving
or running, in the kitchen paring

vegetables for a soup, I whistle the tune,
and cut myself—my thumb instead of
an onion—the blood rushes along

old wild roads, without my effort.

Reunion

My father cautioned us about a fire in the night.
Kick the windows out, jump safe into the woods
just outside the glass, where trees tell their tall dark secrets.

Years later in L.A., I slept and didn't sleep. Outside
a blue light rained over the lot of parked cars.
My heart raced as I woke and bled all night.

All day we had circled the precious place,
every spiral leading to another strange house.
Might that have been the field? those the trees?

The motel curtains veiled a heat I had forgotten.
On the first day of school here, I had all wrong clothes.
A friendly girl asked me what was my middle school,

but no possible answer was the right one.
I sweated my way through the end of that day.
The place sprang into flame, gleaming, untouchable.

In that room gray with smothered light I rose once more.
It might as well have been another country: plaza fountain,
primary school bells, patina of dolphins leaping,

the breathing eucalyptus, the long road to the cliffs and the sea.
I'd thought this place a shrine, a part of the cell lore:
I'd known its scent on my skin, but nothing here knew me.

Hours before time to rise, I rinsed my hands and face.
A stranger scuffed by my door. No windows to open,
I lay down again to twist and burn some more.

Station

panis coelicus
figuris terminum:

In the cathedral, kneeling, I hear a penitent
whisper the prayers of this religion,
finding a way back to God. Above us both,

the light falls, vivid and shimmering.
In one tableau, the angels at the feet
of the Blessed Mother wear robes of green and red,

their wings peridot, pyracantha berry.
In another, the arc of angel wings
over the little Family sheds yods of flame,

bright beatitude, leaves from a fiery tree.
In my native religion, angels do not
have wings in color, nor wings at all.

I learned such attributes as pagan embroideries.
Angels do not cross species, are not fantastic
like griffins or unicorns. They are men and women,

as you and I, but with no blood,
and exalted. Though, as I came here today,
even the birds drew nearer than usual.

The iridescent pigeons spread their wings
at my feet before they lifted into flight,
a little blackbird too, with a red eye

at the place where the wing fans out
from the body. A voice is close by,
waiting to be distilled from the vapor of the air.

Sometimes I can hear a word of it
when I am awakened by the whir of hummingbirds,
something calling my name into stillness.

March

All day, the thread stitching the spangles
to the woolly sky has come unloosed.
Some current moves it at a slant, but otherwise
unhurried and without force it falls.

At the window the blades of the blinds
graph its glimmer, its descent.
I like to hold it whole.
The neighbor still lights his Christmas wreath,

his white-starred topiaries, mid February,
and mugho pines illuminate their dim torchières.
From November till now, how many dogs
have misplaced their barks?

Dark haunched, white chested, this one assumes
a bulldog stance, his growl burring
in a voiceless throat. Let this drifting take its time,
as the unseen bird calls, beagle bays,

gutter collects its fliptops
and soda cans, darker and wetter.
At six, there's a flare in the western gloom,
and still at northern walks,

and at north-faced walls, a white dust of it
persists, and still an icy slip where I walk.
Let the next thing hold its peace.
Let it fall, little by little.

Let the pale cipher plume, let these paillettes
gleam and melt, where the poplars,
shorn in autumn, still shoot skyward, and the leaves
that never fell in a warmer-

than-usual winter still cling,
like dumb, still swallows.

The Debt

The woman down the cat food aisle—long skirt,
hiking boots—dances to the piped-over music.
Tomorrow's the Sabbath, the Mormons
finishing their shopping at quarter to midnight.
She's here, there, spaghetti sauce, soda.
I have the loaf of white bread my son
hollered up the stairs for, which he'll break
into a sacrament at nine a.m.
Finally, in the check-out line, I know her:
she's Kathy's sister, each of us having survived her
now for more than twenty-five years.

We don't say hello. The sister's hair's gray.
In the parking lot I see she drives a big
Republican car as she walks loose-limbed,
California-style, hooded through midnight snow,
with family-size sacks of cereal, gallons of milk.
Beneath the towering parking lot lamps,
the snow falls in pyramids of light.

•

Seeing her breaks the seal between now
and seventeen when, stunned at the fact
of Kathy gone, I never asked: why a death
by a fire of her own making? In some box,
I must still have a folded page of poems
she gave me, written in rosy ink.
Home from the store, I can't stop wondering
if this or if that, which makes my desk

and everything else a clutter, and also me
susceptible to certain viruses of the past
—I could take to bed over unpaid debts
little and great, old thoughtlessness,
toxins with no apparent tincture or cure.
Finally, what have I made of her? The ivy
has snakcd its way inside my window—
it actually points a viney finger at me. So:

shall I tidy up? On my desk two bottles sit,
of paint thinner, of water, one flammable,
one for dousing. The brushes' bristles bend
like old brooms, and I can make new marks,
stroke through paint, drag this ashy debris
just so far, and then new colors will take over.
For a quarter century, in truth,
it's mostly been easy to forget her—so young then,
we scarcely apprehended one another—
but tonight she burns for me anew.

The virtue of disorder is surprise, such as:
a month and a half after Christmas,
finespun threads of angel hair,
like we used to twine around the nativity,
and sheets of tissue with glitter shards
set in the paper whispers. And outside the window,
the steps and tracks dusted, feathered, papered,
layers—that's the snow—and more layers of it still,
the old discarded things baffled, gleaming.

Litany

I dreamed I washed my hair in ash.

At vigil, a forgotten light.
The dog lay at the open door
where the air spoke from the trees.
Nothing—no intruder, no late child.

In the music of that hour,
fan ticking overhead
in an unwritten rhythm, crickets surging,
last or first highway cars,

I dreamed I wore the white dress,
my lap embroidered in fig leaves
where I held the book of my beseeching.
The wood smelled of stain and varnish.

This is my prayer: the curtains
at the window breathe.
A spirit caught between out and in.

At lauds I bathed, dried my skin
with a white towel, dressed
in the clothes I had prepared.
I waited in gray light,

hands unlaced at my belly, fans
crossed there lightly as if holding the ache

would ease it: the porch light burnt out,
the street dark as if it might stay dark all day.

Ave

This is what I want to understand, this
contemplate: drinking bitterness,

but sweetness nonetheless in the midst.
A branch of almond breaks into flower and leaf.

I remember now the mystery
of incarnation, the god entering a body:

as I let him take me, let him lift me up,
let him consume me, satisfy, for those hours,

his longing at my body, let light fall there,
and then the dark, let his smoke fill

my mouth and hair, let him be the god for me:
I learnt the true god, true body,

at his hands: behold! the Christ lifted up
and lain down, tenderly washed

by a woman's hair, with green oils anointed
in their ripe perfumes, rosemary and cloves

folded into his winding sheets; and,
upon rising, discovering his absence

again and again in the centuries,
the callas waiting to hear once more his call:

Occasional Music

The moon is not at all filled up with herself
in my window, nor with the snow

that sweeps by in a stinging cadenza,
wholly improvised, uncoded.

The snow is not at all like the moon,
whose measured sliver, austere, precise,

has emptied herself without fail
for this month end. My child has remarked

all of this, or most of it, as we lie in the dark,
early, before the delivery of the paper,

before the first workers arise, before they drink
orange juice or slice thick bread for toast.

He and I are the earliest observers,
though he has fallen asleep again

in my arms, his mouth with its own weather,
the small breath still sweet in sleep.

I grieve him and look at the moon,
my fierce commonplace: I parse her out,

full, halved, quartered, whittled now
away to nothing, though the storms

of an oncoming winter play on:
furioso, appassionata.

Salvage

I peel red potatoes, grainy and sweet.
As usual I improvise, to make a salad
of asparagus, sliced leeks, a roasted red pepper
salvaged from the moment
it might have gone bad, but not quite.

I douse all this with a green olive oil,
expensive vinegar, salt it, pepper it,
in faith that it will compose a supper,
that my children will eat and grow strong.
I've made rolls with hard cornmeal crusts,

an x slashed into each. The air blooms
with heat and steam, wild yeast and wheat,
onions, peppers, each odor in ascendancy
or decline as the evening goes forward.
Because it's Sunday, I'm thinking about

how happiness can be wrung from suffering;
how, since for half the year, my children live
with their father, now this pang at their fleeting arrivals.
At the window, a tentative sun lowers into,
pinks the spring clouds. I feel scrupulous,

twist hot water from the rag, mop the counter clean.
My two oldest nap in their rooms
as I finish the supper they'll eat together,
quarrel briefly over, and at night, sleep upon.

•

Later, I have begun to put it away.

After supper, after they've gone, in the last of the evening
—the air streaming in through a window—
I feel the summer coming on. I rinse plates,
scour spoons and forks, leave pans to soak.
I see the children sleeping, fading

into nightfall, and before I fall into my own night,
the moon will stream in the slatted window,
pattern a bright grid in the corner's shadow, and I
will think of the stories we tell about death now—
a dark stem, through which we walk toward a rose of light.

Dog Aria

Late, when the sprinklers came on,
I'd find myself listening at the window
for our dachshund, ever surprised
into song by the slosh of dishes,
late loads of laundry—his quick

sprechgesang matching the water's
gush and spray. He had perfect pitch,
and as the yard got wetter and wetter,
he swam among staves of delphinium
and sweet bergamot, baying at a border

of lemon verbena, his frisky yipe
an allegro of catmint. His elegant snout
lifted to the moon. Each night he unveiled
from his blankets the dog-and-a-half
of his body into the dark rapt air,

and from his big chest, his rapid heart,
he drew the leitmotif of dog, of night,
and the long notes, impossibly long—
Tonight, a draft stirs the garden, quiet
and tuneless:
                O scenter, hunter—O song!

Flowering Tobacco

I could sleep now, I am almost drunk with sleepiness.
The sweet night flower with its seamed petals,

the little throat of its center drinks up light:
nicotiana, late and vivid, gleaming in its wet bed.

The dianthus, single-flowered carnation,
bunches and bends to the weather, its core of clove

still willing to rise at the touch. In this last
ecstasy of noticing, first these salmon flowers;

then the apricot, warm in a child's palm,
taken right from the tree; last, its flat pit,

later, on the table by the door. The warm nights
under the same cold moon. The last couple of crickets

make their brave and unconsoling song,
its little interval. And then, the slipping of this moment

into what's next: the drying grasses in the lot
at the edge of the park. The empty branches of flowers.

The husks of bees lying still in corners, on the sills.
It is only a small song, when things die for the year;

yet when I go out into the night falling earlier and earlier,
waiting for dark to consume me, I can't tell

if the lull of the insects is a failing, or if
it is the single song left to me, just hearing it,

just the last sexual odor of the lawn, just being
there when rain clouds swallow up the sky.

Tell Me Why

The hand of the husband on his wife's breast
falls away in the rain of her indifference.
He turns again in their barren sleep,
dreams of her cool face, of the orchids
that ring the fingers of her left hand

now that the ring itself has disappeared.
She adores a shadowy god whose form
changes without warning, who bears
no resemblance to the genial gods
of their youth, who smiled upon the conceptions

and births of their many children. He sees her
at an altar, hears the strange voice piercing
a voice he thought he knew. Once
his hands on her skin made her body sing in praise.
Now his hands pray alms. Her eyes

are transparent, her once soft arms
hawk's wings; her skin smells of pine fire.
He sees her at the window, which she unlocks
every night. One night he knows he'll find her print
on the casement, her shadow blackening the moon.

The Undoing

If it were my bed and my house, I'd turn
my hand to undoing. I'd strip the bedding
and blankets away, and unquilt the mattress
and shred the tick. The shoes I'd take
out of the closet, ready for the feet
leaving the house in pairs, in pairs of pairs.
Sweaters we'd no longer need, since it's summer
and we've ended our talk of the cold; and so
out of the drawers they'd come, and the drawers, too,
the chests with their naked ribs. At the basin,
I'd leave the bar of soap, half dissolved
from our hands' washings. Someone else may think
of cleanliness. Out of the box would come the rings,
earrings, necklaces of encircling affection;
I'd open the windows to make my hand more free
in letting fall the glittering things to the lawn below.
Out of albums would fall photographs, leaves

of an unsewn book. Even the socks with undarned holes
in their heels—these I'd unravel, stitch by minute stitch:
domestic details that have prophesied
their own demise; I'd fulfill their promise.
And the children, the ones who sleep in the beds!
I am wondering what to do with them:
every day they are taller, longer, like tadpoles
changing form in water, a dart and a wriggle,
a disappearing fin, the last vestige of a tail; then
a muscled thigh, an exact inventory of toes.
These, too: their shirts and shoes now fail them,
flattened into the baskets into which
I layered them, sundering, unweaving.
While they sleep, best to dismantle: clean it out.
Open doors, open windows. Let the night,
let nothing but air inhabit these rooms.

Self-Portrait as Half of Herself

Mother finding the daughter now mute
in the late summer ripeness of nameless plums;
in the way the grapes fall into hand,
all their sugar heavy and blooming
on the dusky skins; in the wine-odor
of falling petals from spent roses;
in the shimmer of gnats low on the lawn
cool over applefall: at the early hour,

easier to ignore her
plangent face, the brow of her turning
away, because I was listening
so intently for the soft dirt broken
by the insistent, whispering leaves
of plain beans, but she is there—there is no doubt
—she grieves that mother who helplessly
let her go, let her sow herself
into the ground as common seed,
as any ordinary pathos,
so unremarkable that it has been flayed
of its proper salt.

        I have dreamed her
the brave girl heroine of a horror film,
but softer, her start as I wake
not of terror but sorrow, the sorrow
hinted at in our life within time,
when I go out before the light has broken
through the trees, into a garden full of seed,
turned dirt, absent the weeds, absent yet
the luxurious weeds, and as if the air
were holding its breath—

Door

—incised etched embossed I painted it

     the black of broad strokes in all colors   each

stroke canceling another   impasto rune

     without key   and now I wait at its threshold

and none of my deceit nor stealth can breach it

     this door founded on a rock: though I made it

of the noise of divers hands   my knock on this

     now so still this so somber relic of a door

yields nothing: a token I hid I think I hear

     on its other side bristling   a commotion

and a goad: having salvaged it   I should

     embrace it: I press against battened light

to hear its ardent sealed unsayable name—

Hymn

I have said I would linger years in stifling attic rooms
with a pen in my hand and dingy paper in readiness
for your voice to speak itself through my lips

but instead I have not waited at all, you've not
sulked at my unworthiness or the shambling wreck
of this room, my life. And in the place of all sullenness

you have brought me a splendor of gifts,
have left the window open so that cool autumn air
pours perpetually in, stirring the still atoms,

and you have waked me in the night, murmured my name
which none other may hear, and have pressed yourself
on me, over me, your hair falling, dark star.

You have shown me the road to the river, then to the sea;
you have urged me on to the door so that I will depart
into air stinging like wine in the throat.

I have found cold apples heaped on our bed and have felt
your hand on my skin. I have not needed to court you,
because you love me, my words and voice,

and when I have wept to submit to harsher gods,
you've sung me back to you, in holy words,
ravishing.

Hill Country

The sheets shorn back, my hips at your mouth:

yesterday we bought white peaches
near the Pedernales River, which runs

through the ranch where LBJ lived out the last years
he had the prescience to know would be brief.
Acre after acre he added

to the spread, to console a late despair.
The fruit scents our room, where we've told ourselves
the past is past, in this interval far from home.

A Sunday morning, this hotel room
—we can afford to take it slow,
even though the sky grays with smoke

drifting north from fires burning in Mexico.
Another crisis, this time not ours. Not ours,
the territory, the ranch's soil which,

we were told, derives its dark strength
from the river, its cycle of flood
and decline, flood and decline.

No erosion, despite the fitful havoc—
just laden trees and a profusion of blooms:
evening primrose, bluebonnet,

wrinkled poppy, black-eyed Susan, thistle,
wild cosmos, and over all of it,
the birds fly, swoop and dive.

We'll take our cue from them, the peaches
now spilling from their flimsy sack. You'll lift

your face to me, move up and over me nearer,
your lips and beard stained with juice,
the pulp and flesh of your tasting, eating.

At Midnight

I'm on dark streets, damp and shining, music still in my throat
as the trees' arms dim, the moon rises, the street lights

flare and fade at their intervals, and even diehard
nightowls are throwing back the last of the wine,

starting to wash, going to bed, alone or next to sleeping lovers:
I drive with the radio still on, waiting for the smooth talk

to end, for the sax to rise, for that lonely trumpet,
for the travelers to begin their slow caravan; for the sliding down,

the falling off, the loosening, unfastening: I'm waiting
for more music and more unsung unspoken language,

improvised, to fill the hour when I might be clasped
deep into the heart of my home if I wished it, but I do not,

not yet: think of me, then, freed only in the dark hours by this
late jazz. Think of me as you drift off, tuned to that same

station, the strand of that same unknotted string slipping
over your undone body, pearl by gleaming pearl.

The Bats of Congress Avenue

The bats beneath the Congress Avenue Bridge
comprise the largest colony in North America.
We know this, since one night,
hours after they'd flown, we walked down
by the winding lake, near the kiosk
which also said how gentle and yet wild
these bats, Talarida brasiliensis,
coming out by the thousands at dusk
to forage and feed. The legend said
not to fear them, though the idea
of their dark roost, their soft chatter
as they sleep, growing louder as they stir

at cool evening—is this not the heart
of the uncanny? Earlier, at the hour of flight,
we were verging on the body's own dusk,
nearer to the dark-on-dark of caves, the under-
places, silkiest skin, untended hair,
the unlooked-for arc where shoulder
joins arm and torso, where a folded hand fits,
ball in socket, the way a bat folds its
leather and bone wings into itself:
my hand there the way yours unfolds itself
inside me, dim harbor at evenfall,
before we fly again by ear into the dark.

Guide to Bird Life and Behavior

It winters in Mexico and Costa Rica

We think we saw the drab girl
    at the springs yesterday, tracing
    lemniscates in the sky before swooping
down to the water with the swallows.

Why does the male dress so beautifully
    to mate? That's one question, and another:
    why did we see them only the one summer,
these *not uncommon birds* that seemed

to have an agreement with the osprey
    trying to keep the site of its nest
    undisclosed, circling in brawny
but not flashy flight while the tanager

distracted us with its red head,
    its yellow neck and breast, sitting
    helpfully on this then that branch.
Then a brilliant speedy hum of bird

rending the chasm to the flowing water.
    What was its business there?
    We saw an eagle take fish from the river,
the caterpillars swarm their sticky silk,

on this path I've walked every summer
    since I was a child. Honestly,
    I'm not sure the bird is what I think it is.
We looked it up in the field guide. Western

Tanager is our best guess, and it seems
        apt that the book describes the bird
        as *secretive* (its red head
will fade in the fall). —What vivid dreams I had

in the familiar bed, I'll never tell. Back home, a robin
        alights frankly on the closest branch,
        with only a window bordered in ivy
and a small enigma between us.

Limit

It is the afternoon after. At the pool,
the children shriek, and glissandi of water
lift and fall, hang in the air, circulate
through the grass, over bare skin.

The clouds pass before the sun, an intermittent
diminishing. I soak up heat and light, soak up
the drifting of the clouds, take in
the pattern of the breeze sweeping the sweat

off my skin. If only it were something less personal,
more abstract, the me in this afternoon,
then I'd know what to make of this,
not merely wish for the last of summer

to burn away what's come apart inside.
Then I wouldn't say, trying for dispassion,
this is something resembling heartbreak.
I'd know how to read the languages of birds

crossing my path. For the last three days,
they've come near, two hummingbirds,
fawn-colored hoverers, one in the canyon,
another by the stream; then a bluejay,

diving across the road. Wholly in the flesh,
or nearly, I'd let their flight brush my skin.

The body, the body: I say it as if
it were the name of a deliverer,

some new thing from which to learn
the hard lesson of limits, when
I am spent and still full of longing:
what takes me, then says, here—no further.

The Blade

Dark, and I wake with the keen breath
of a dream's blade at my neck, its faint chill.
Press my eyes, press back memory, desire's throb,
the blood in its thick blue vein.

Start writing, but I'm watched thrice over:
he loved watching me touch myself, open my thighs,
bring myself to pulse under my own hand: then
enter, panting. But this time we aren't alone—

a child, not his, not mine, watches us watch one another,
watches me write on the page. A he
and a she perform there, roughly corresponding,
I guess, to him and me—but now also this boy, a waif,

I'm tempted to call him, sentimentally, who squats
on the curb, elbows on knees and chin in hands,
looking at nothing in particular—but maybe at them.
In the sleep called eros we're always alone,

locked in a room where we've made a high kingdom of a bed,
of white sheets, the sheen of sweat on his body
and mine, the magnet of our connecting parts. I think
I've never dreamed, never written, this child:

or have always drawn the curtain, as I do now,
against him, against his feet in the gutter water,
against the heedless water rushing. Wake and write,
wake and write, now shut out the daylight

pressing against the curtain, against the child's eyes'
squint: he can't see us, nor into our solitary locked empire,
but sees instead the nothing we leave behind,
since we dream away in a room where we reign and reign.

I am driving home from the hospital

   where my son is, where his veins swim
in the water he's lost and he sleeps till they come
for more of his blood; after this, the dark god,

the one whose name is on the altar, the one
who demands sacrifice, broken hearts, contrition,
that god of this world seizes me

in a cold grip, and says to me,
you believed that you could have
whatever it was you wanted, you believed

like a fool in the inhabited moment,
in the full days and nights of desire,
you believed, and what you believed

will be your doom. He says,
believe what you will, but know the law:
that for every moment you took,

for every day and night that you filled
with an urge, with longing, it will be
one moment of pain for those you have loved.

Tonight it is your blond boy on the altar.
He says to me, you have stopped listening
to the voice of justice, you've been a thief

in my house, and you will pay. But,
he says, not from your own
pocket. Take the coin from the boy.

Envoi

> An abandoned suit weighs so much on the shoulders
>
> Lorca

With my car in reverse, I hit the stray cat
I'd named after the poet and fed for weeks,
and as I held his broken body,
laid him in a box,
buried it under the empty pear tree,
as I scrubbed the blood from the drive,
the sky dark and darkening, as I fell
to the bed under which a dog
was eating my shoes,

the miserable letters my soul was writing daily
loosened themselves from the folio
my ribs had made for them,

posted themselves like the new translations
I read and wanted, briefly, to send you,
your absence seeding itself everywhere—
a glare in the glass, warm brick walls,
the plaid jacket of the man at the freeway exit.

This radiant October still blooms asters and roses,
but tastes of coffee, semen, ash.

Notes toward elergy

That day I imagined him in flames, the day I heard of his death,
the cat on my table batted the dying lilacs, the florets barely
clinging to the stem by brittle threads, falling blue & gray
like ash. Falling to the table like a pool of blue ash. Thinking,
yes, this, his fabled excesses, it could be fire, emblem enough,
knowing now that it's just the words left of him, just the ashes.
To let his language inhabit me for awhile, pass through me like
wind through sheer fabric; grazing me, lifting up the curtain &
passing by, repeatedly; tearing through the house of me in sheets
of flame. Putting on the clothing of his language, hoping to
take on charisma in the praising & the mourning of him.   Not
enough, of course: not enough grief & not enough language to
meet the fact of him smoking outside the building. Not enough
to match the voice of him saying, Members of the Committee
on the Ineffable, or him sitting elbows on the table, bored but
patient, listening to some poet translate another dream. Once I
saw him outside a laundromat, holding a woman & kissing her
on his motorcycle. What are lilacs or a petulant cat to that seedy
& therefore eloquent romance? A cat who never even knew
him, for that matter? I am like one of the necessary though
mute figures Chekhov imagined for a Russian novel in a last late
fragment: a parrot; a thrush; a dog so clever he can practically
speak. & doggedly I insist, I insist I will make an elegy out of
this brief chapter, out of laundry if I must, out of something as
ordinary as dishtowels or socks, lank hair, startling eyes; out of
his belly in his shirt, his slouch; improvising something out of
this too much life, now absent even his poor things. Moorless, I
keep banging up against whatever presents itself, as on Memorial
Day, when we looked for my husband's grandfather's grave,
finding myself standing in the cemetery on Prospect Avenue.
The addresses of the dead. & then up a little hill, where a doe
nosed the wall, & a rabbit ran across the small apartments where

they lay sleeping. This Arcadia. He returns at the last—where?
to the long central valley of California, to flowering & harvest,
cultivation, to mist & miasma. On what street if any does he
live? What animals flank his grave, graze at his bed?

for Larry Levis

Medicine Mountain

Big Horn Mountains, October 2010

In the west *medicine* doesn't mean *dose* or *comfit*.
It means the thing or place believed to have power,

and therefore cure. So when our friend dislodged us
from the truck, and we climbed the remaining hill,

approached the wheel, I expected at least that.
We circumambulated to the left, east, because power

is said to flow that way. The rope fence encircling it
had ribbons and torn fabric, kerchiefs, bundles tied to it.

My amulet hung heavy on my chest,
and with it I took the pictures I needed to see:

on the ground the wheel stretched
away from me, no matter where I stood,

and the earth seemed to curve at the far edge.
I caught the nearest cairn but not the far;

the stones lined up, forming the spokes, seemed
random, not emblematic. I looked west

into some far nation, the whole mountain floor
descending away, rolling, submerged in an ocean of air.

So old—at least centuries—I wondered I'd not heard of it,
and upon inquiry its secrets still held: who made it

is long dead, and who still visits it for purposes
barely written and uncirculated is not saying:

I heard of a man once there, witness to the ceremony,
who found himself floating above the ground.

I heard it might be the lodge where spirits reside,
I heard it might be where the dead are:

Acknowledgments

Many thanks to George Kalamaras for choosing this manuscript. His wise comments helped me as I finished the book. Thanks also to Dana Curtis, and for the labor of love that is Elixir Press. Thanks to my readers, the friends and interlocutors of these poems: Wade Bentley, Ann Cannon, Katharine Coles, Mary Gardner, Kimberly Johnson, Lynn Kilpatrick, Kati Lewis, Paisley Rekdal, Stephen Ruffus, Natasha Saje, Susan Sample, and Jennifer Tonge. Their attentive response helped bring this book into being.

I owe a debt of thanks to my teachers Bruce Jorgensen and Larry Levis. And I am grateful beyond measure to my family, whose love, faith, and unwavering support made writing this work possible. Thanks to John, for always and for everything.

Thanks to the editors of the journals where some of the poems were first published (sometimes in earlier versions):

Sugar House Review: "Sutra"
Caketrain: "Self-Portrait as Half of Herself," "In Taos"
Hunger Mountain Review: "Concord"
Quarterly West: "Girl"
Mudfish: "From a Pastoral"
Frontiers: A Journal of Women Studies: "The Undoing"
Tar River Poetry: "Ring of Fire," "Ave," "The Debt"
Southword.: "Hill Country

"Dog Aria" was a part of the Utah Arts Council's Bite-Size Poem project, and was published as a video on the Web.

"Station" was published (in an earlier version) in *Fire in the Pasture: 21ˢᵗ Century Mormon Poets.*

LISA BICKMORE's poems and video work have appeared in a number of publications, including *Quarterly West, Tar River Poetry, Caketrain, Sugarhouse Review, The Moth, Terrain, Mapping Salt Lake City,* and *Southword.* Among her honors is the Ballymaloe International Poetry Prize for 2015. She is an Associate Professor of English at Salt Lake Community College, where she is also one of the founders of its Publication Center.

TITLES FROM ELIXIR PRESS

POETRY

Circassian Girl by Michelle Mitchell-Foust

Imago Mundi by Michelle Mitchell-Foust

Distance From Birth by Tracy Philpot

Original White Animals by Tracy Philpot

Flow Blue by Sarah Kennedy

A Witch's Dictionary by Sarah Kennedy

The Gold Thread by Sarah Kennedy

Rapture by Sarah Kennedy

Monster Zero by Jay Snodgrass

Drag by Duriel E. Harris

Running the Voodoo Down by Jim McGarrah

Assignation at Vanishing Point by Jane Satterfield

Her Familiars by Jane Satterfield

The Jewish Fake Book by Sima Rabinowitz

Recital by Samn Stockwell

Murder Ballads by Jake Adam York

Floating Girl (Angel of War) by Robert Randolph

Puritan Spectacle by Robert Strong

X-testaments by Karen Zealand

Keeping the Tigers Behind Us by Glenn J. Freeman

Bonneville by Jenny Mueller

Cities of Flesh and the Dead by Diann Blakely

Green Ink Wings by Sherre Myers

Orange Reminds You Of Listening by Kristin Abraham

In What I Have Done & What I Have Failed To Do by Joseph P. Wood

Bray by Paul Gibbons

The Halo Rule by Teresa Leo

Perpetual Care by Katie Cappello

The Raindrop's Gospel: The Trials of St. Jerome and St. Paula by Maurya Simon

Prelude to Air from Water by Sandy Florian

Let Me Open You A Swan by Deborah Bogen

Cargo by Kristin Kelly

Spit by Esther Lee

Rag & Bone by Kathrym Nuernberger

Kingdom of Throat-stuck Luck by George Kalamaras

Mormon Boy by S. Brady Tucker

Nostalgia for the Criminal Past by Kathleen Winter

Little Oblivion by Susan Allspaw

Quelled Communiqués by Chloe Joan Lopez

Stupor by David Ray Vance

Curio by John Nieves

The Rub by Ariana-Sophia Kartsonis

Visiting Indira Gandhi's Palmist by Kirun Kapur

Freaked by Liz Robbins

Looming by Jennifer Franklin

Flammable Matter by Jacob Victorine

Prayer Book for the Anxious by Josephine Yu

flicker by Lisa Bickmore

FICTION

How Things Break by Kerala Goodkin

Juju by Judy Moffat

Grass by Sean Aden Lovelace

Hymn of Ash by George Looney

Nine Ten Again by Phil Condon

Memory Sickness by Phong Nguyen

Troglodyte by Tracy DeBrincat

The Loss of All Lost Things by Amina Gautier